I0468965

Swear Word Coloring Book

MAGICAL BAD BEASTS

SWEAR WORD COLORING BOOK FOR ADULTS

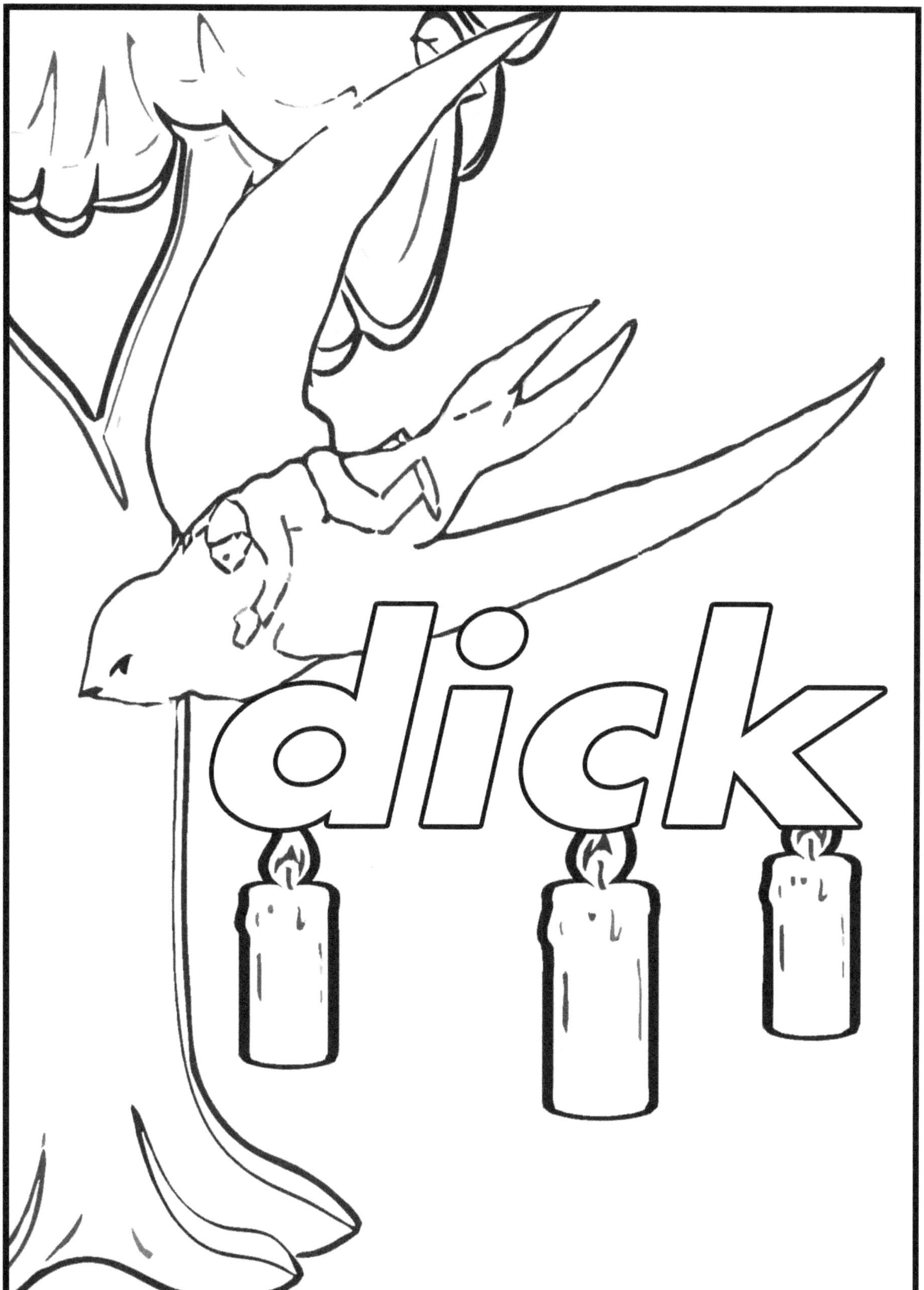
dick

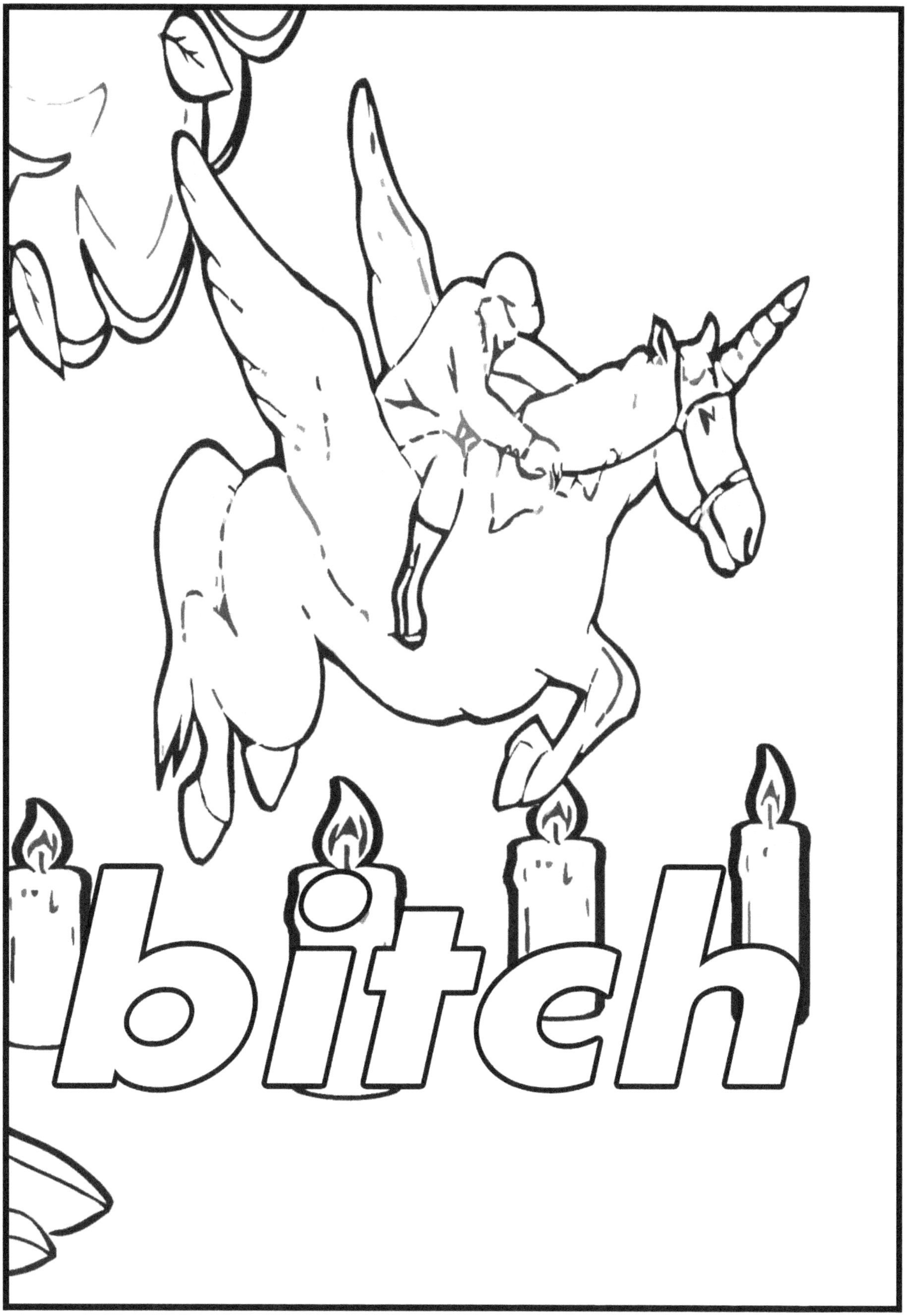
bitch

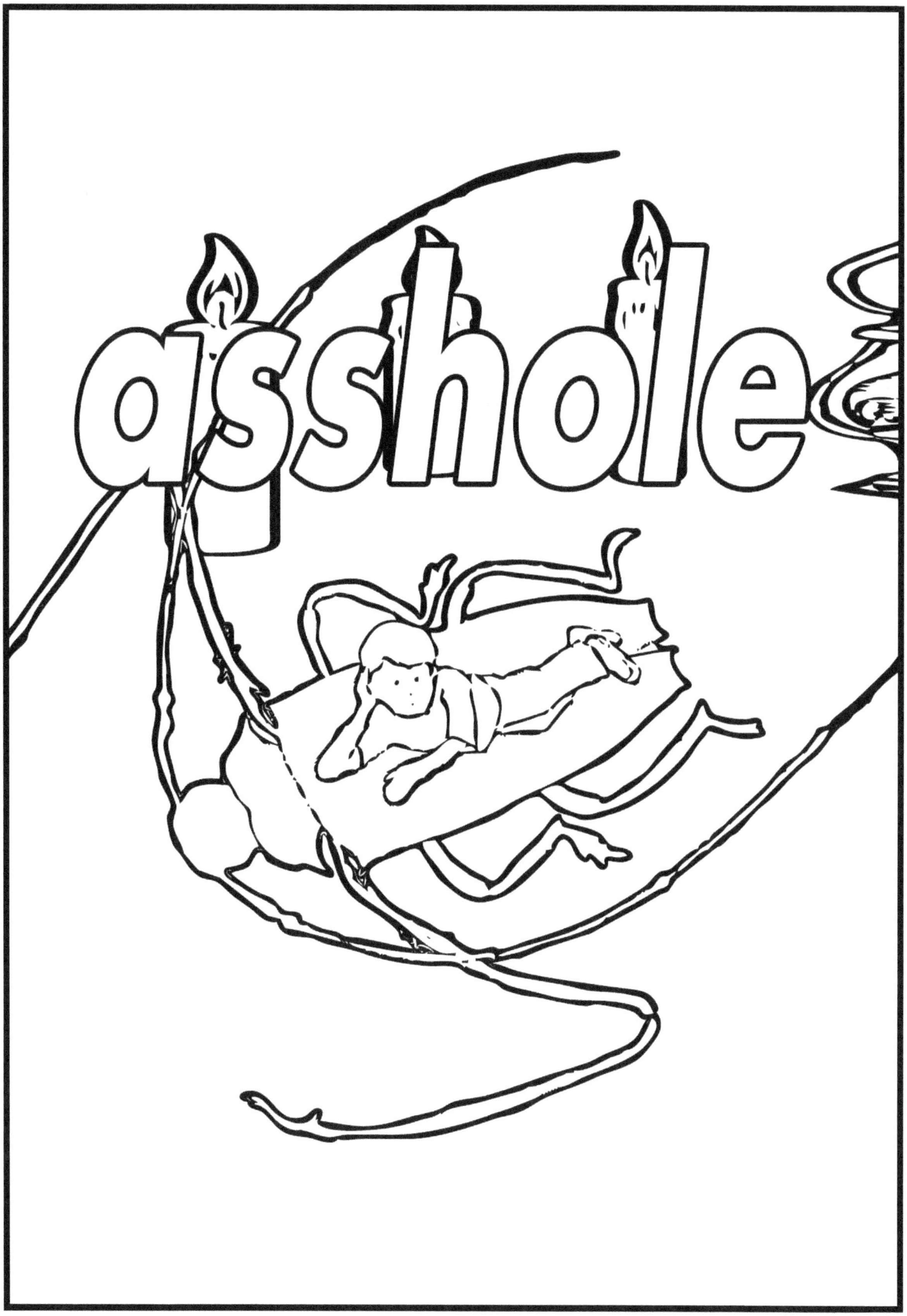
asshole

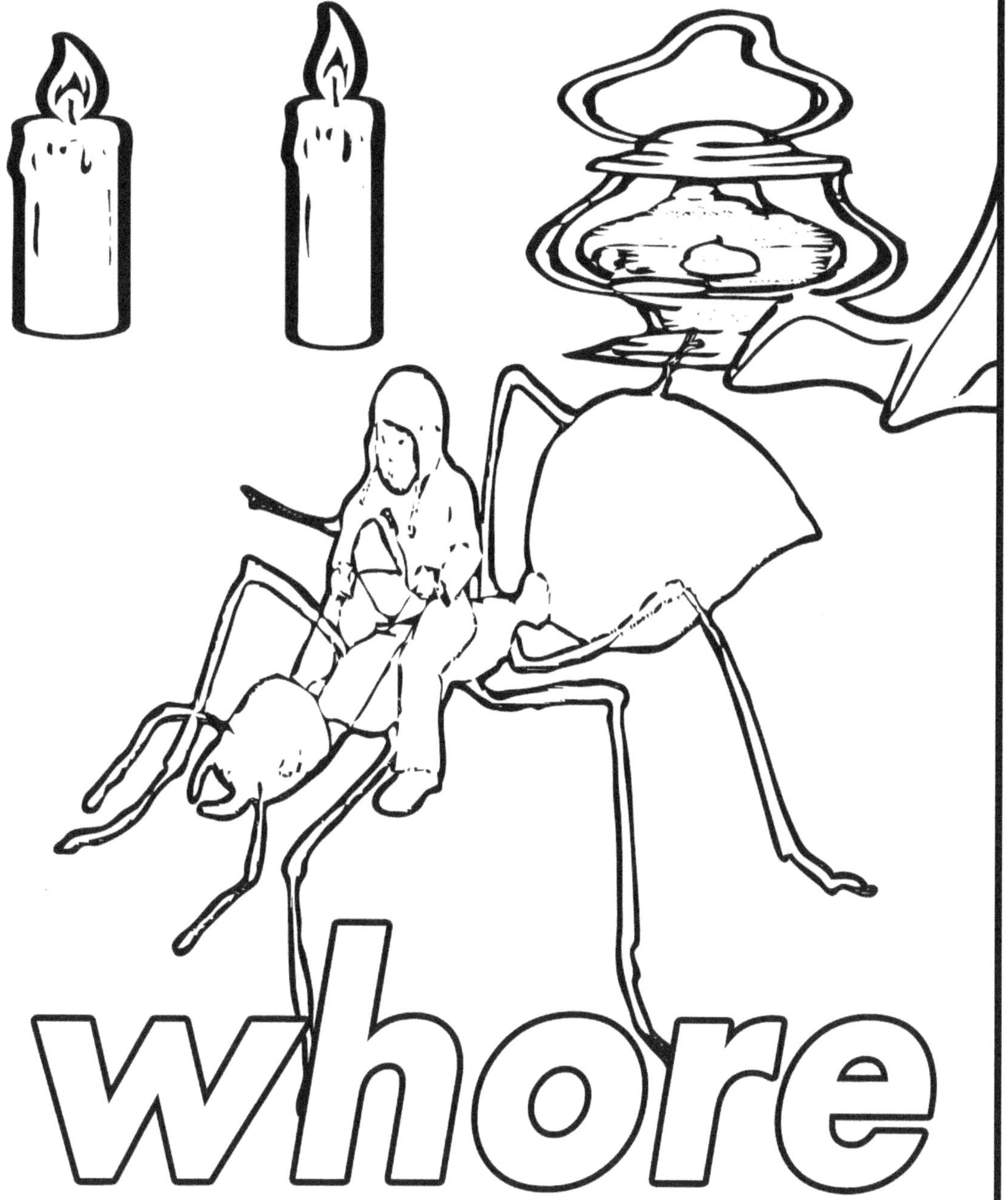

whore

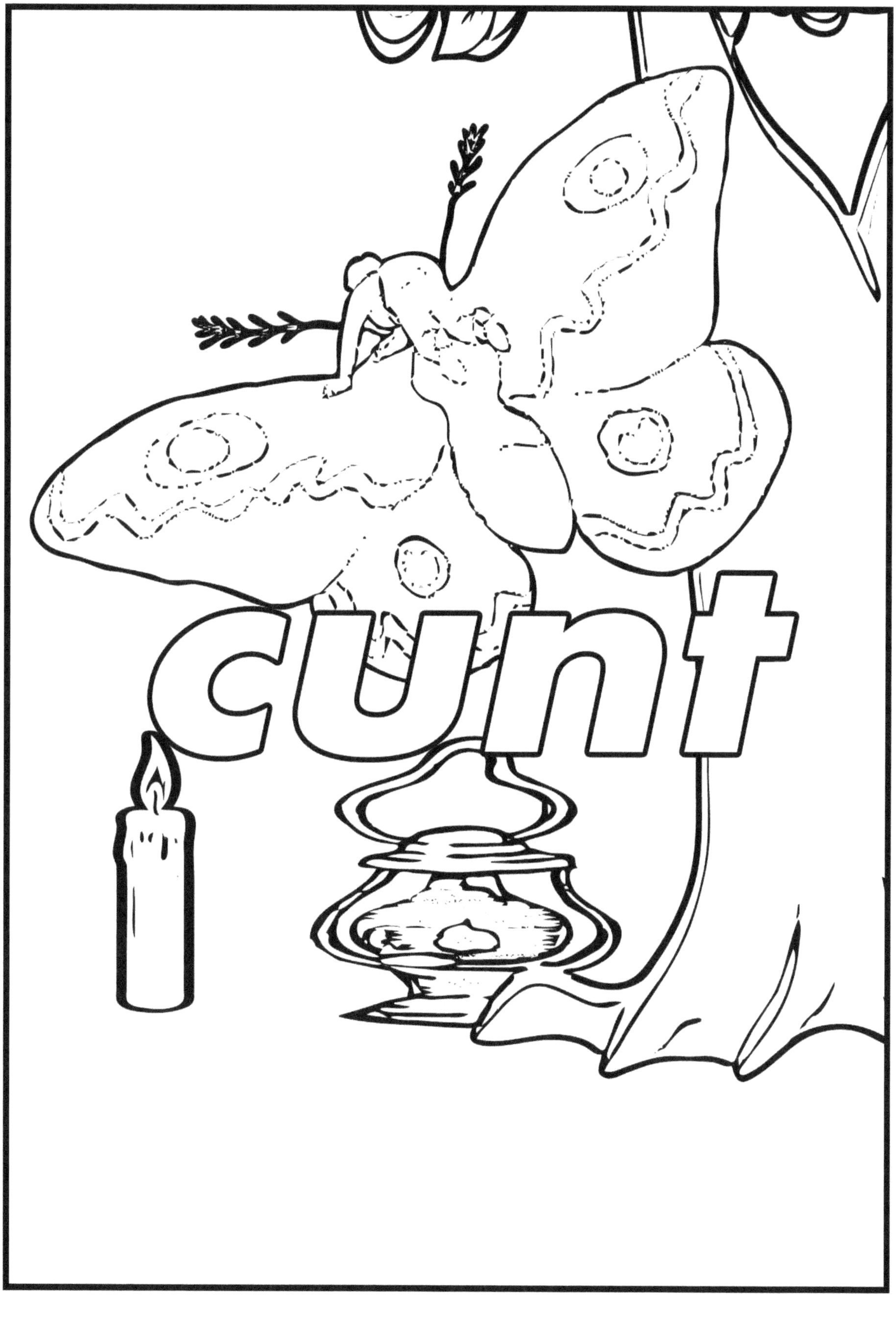
cunt

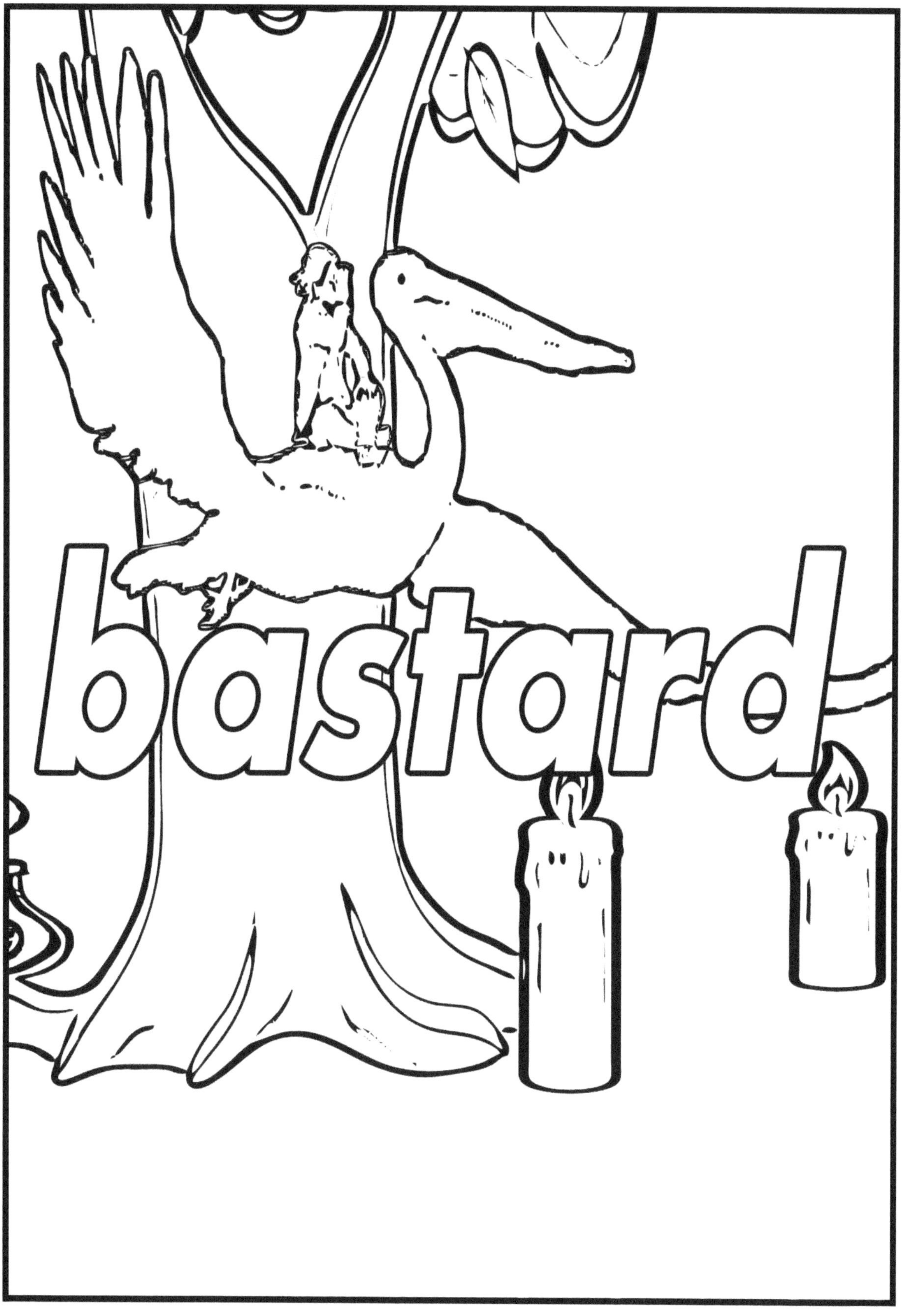
bastard

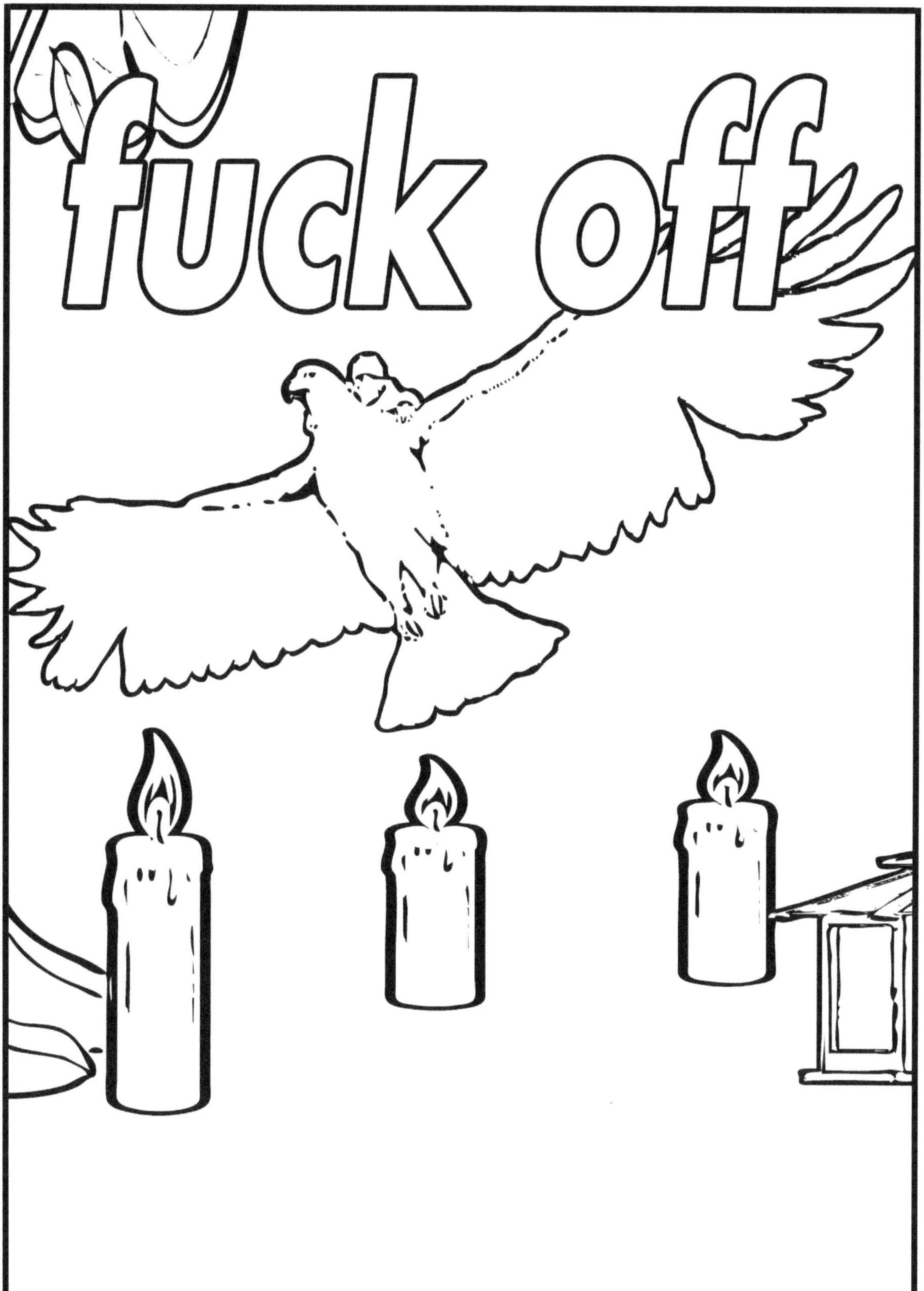
fuck off

big balls

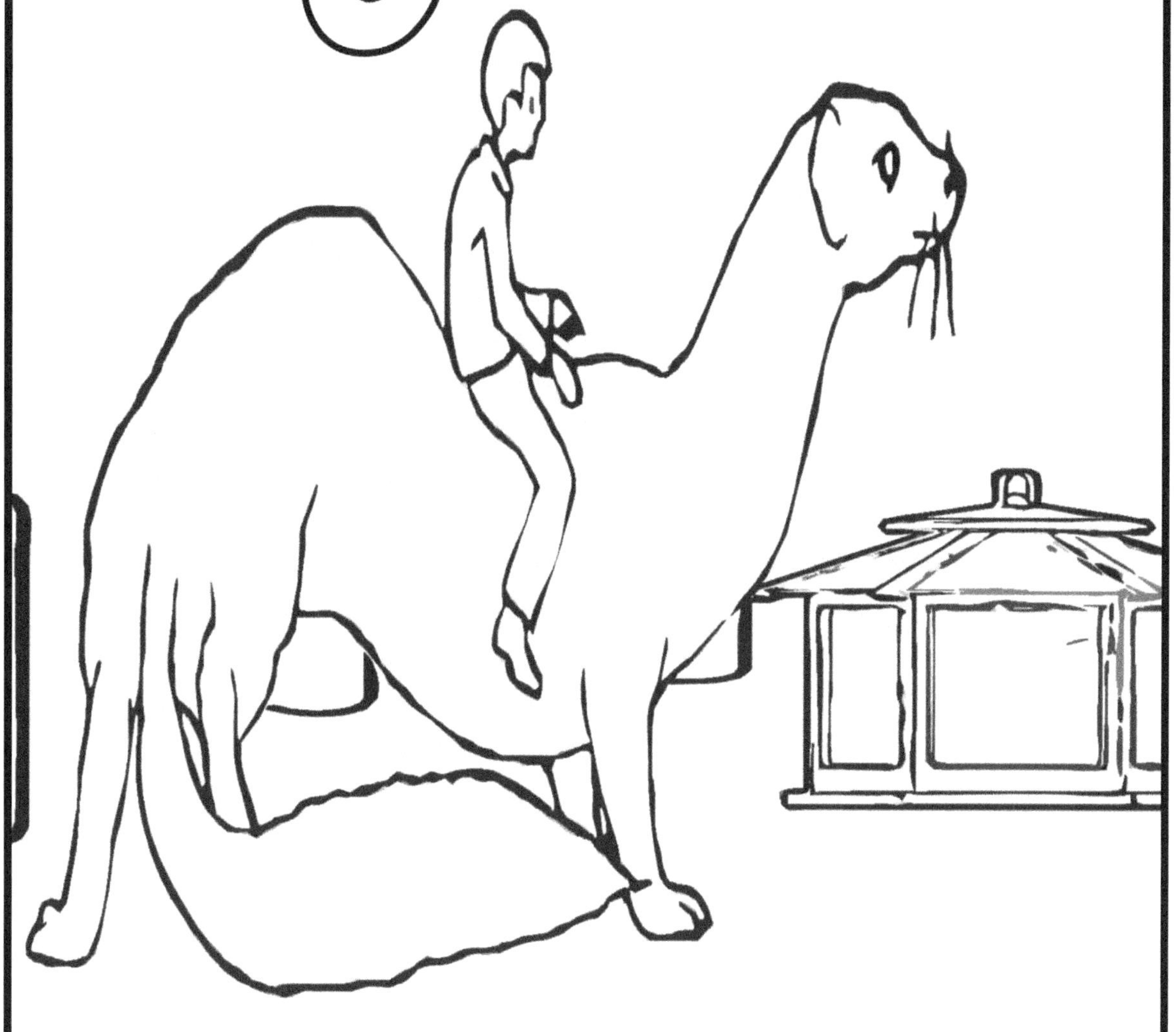

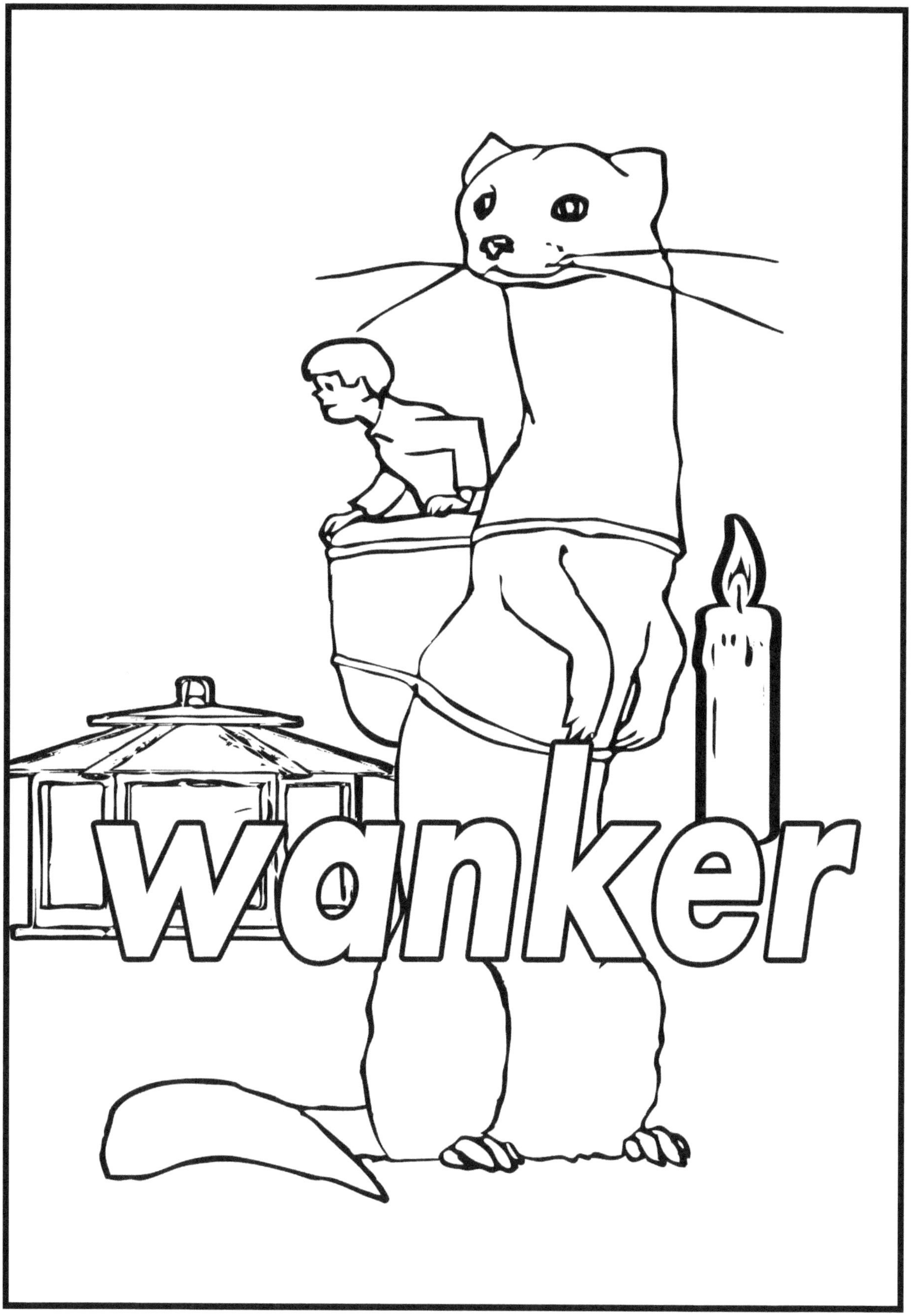
wanker

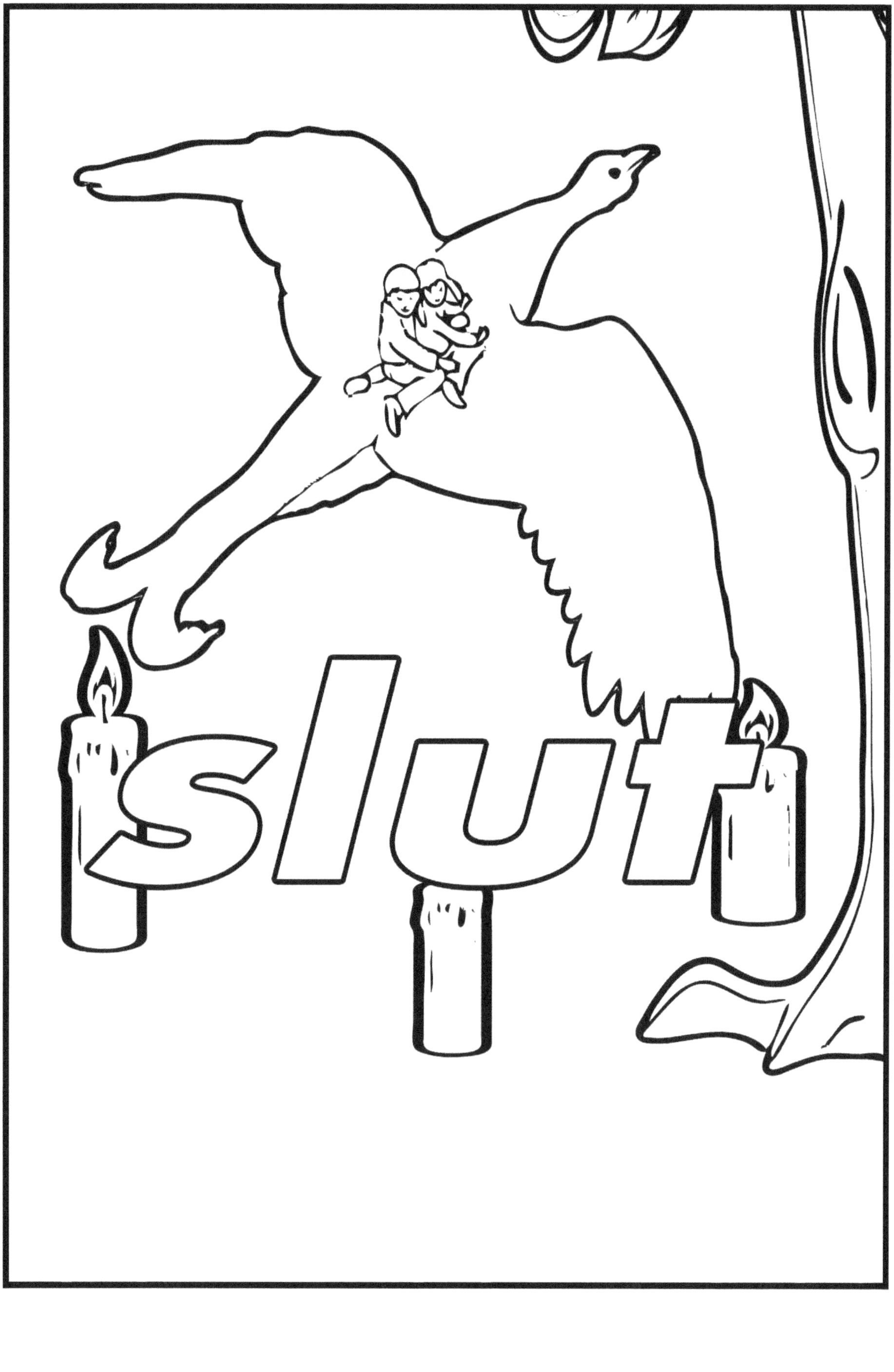
slut

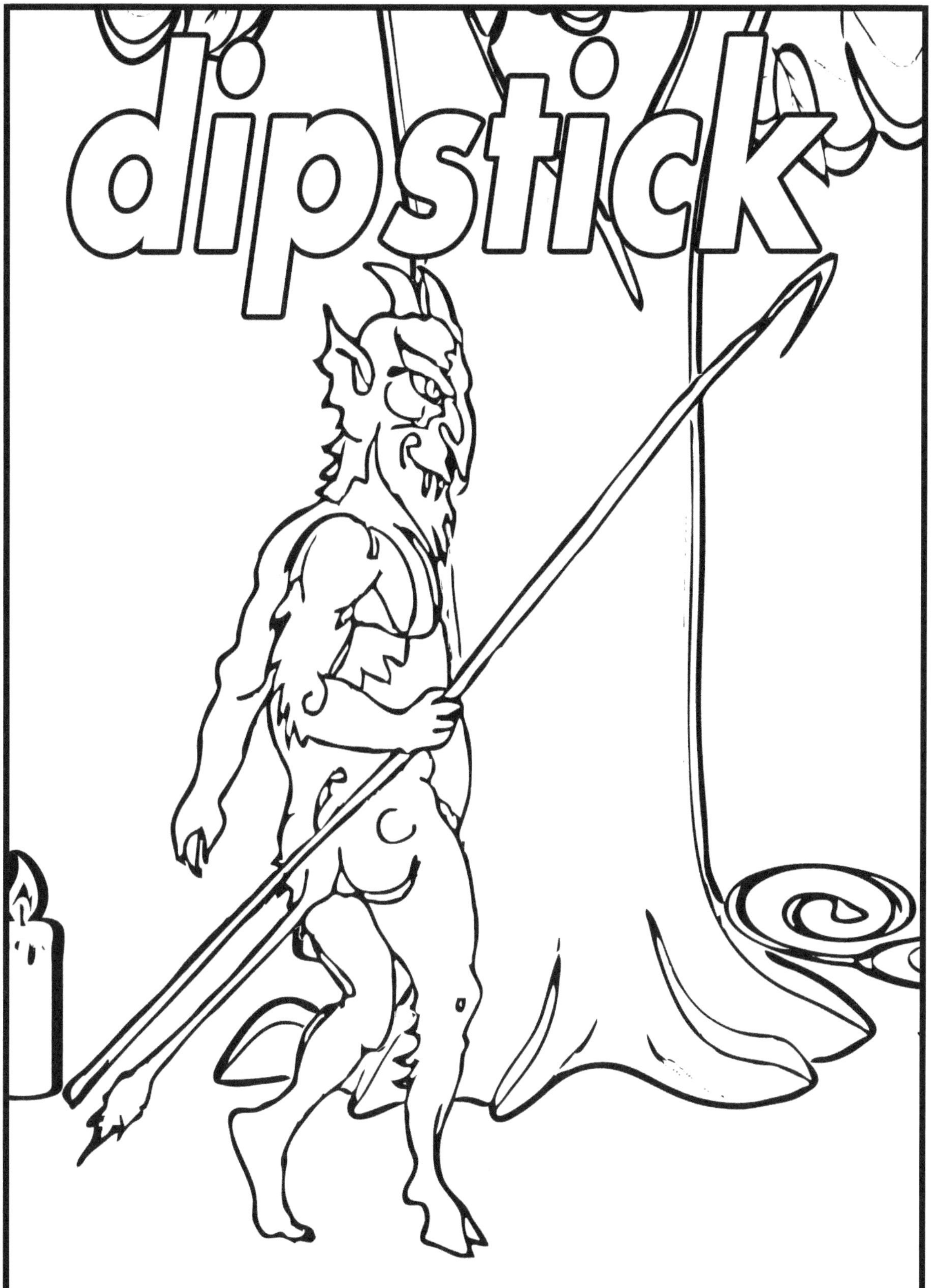
dipstick

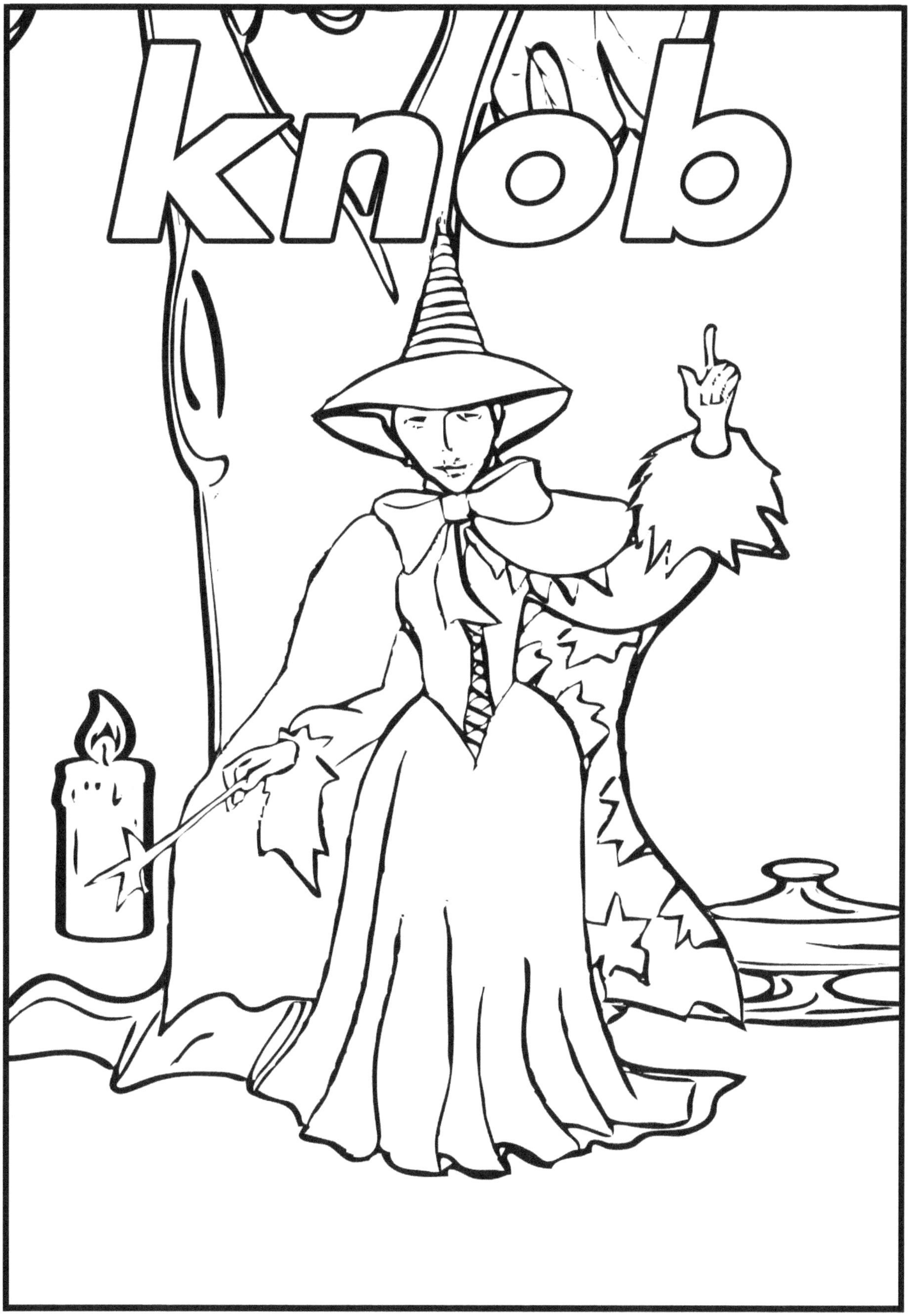
knob

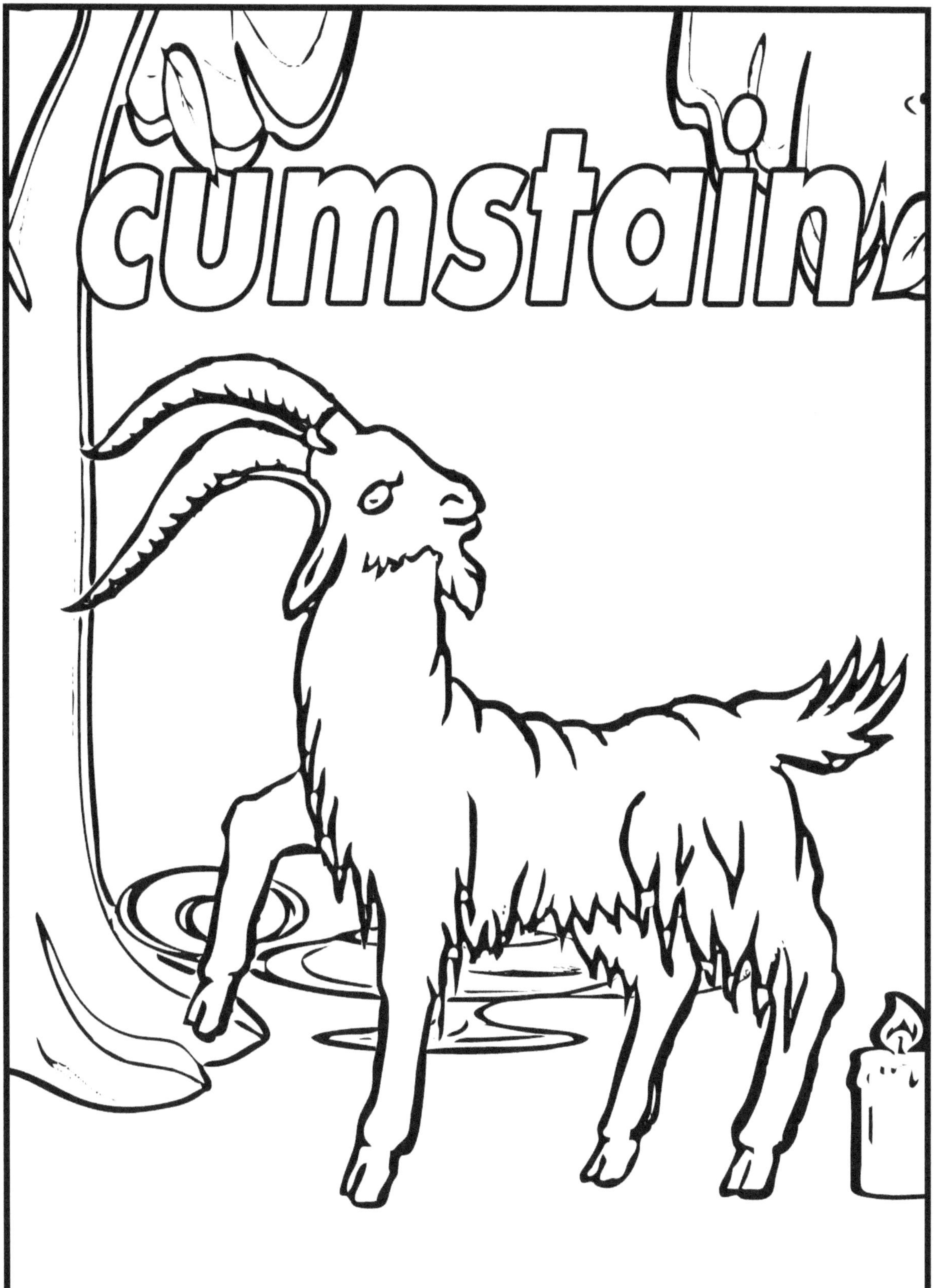
cumstain

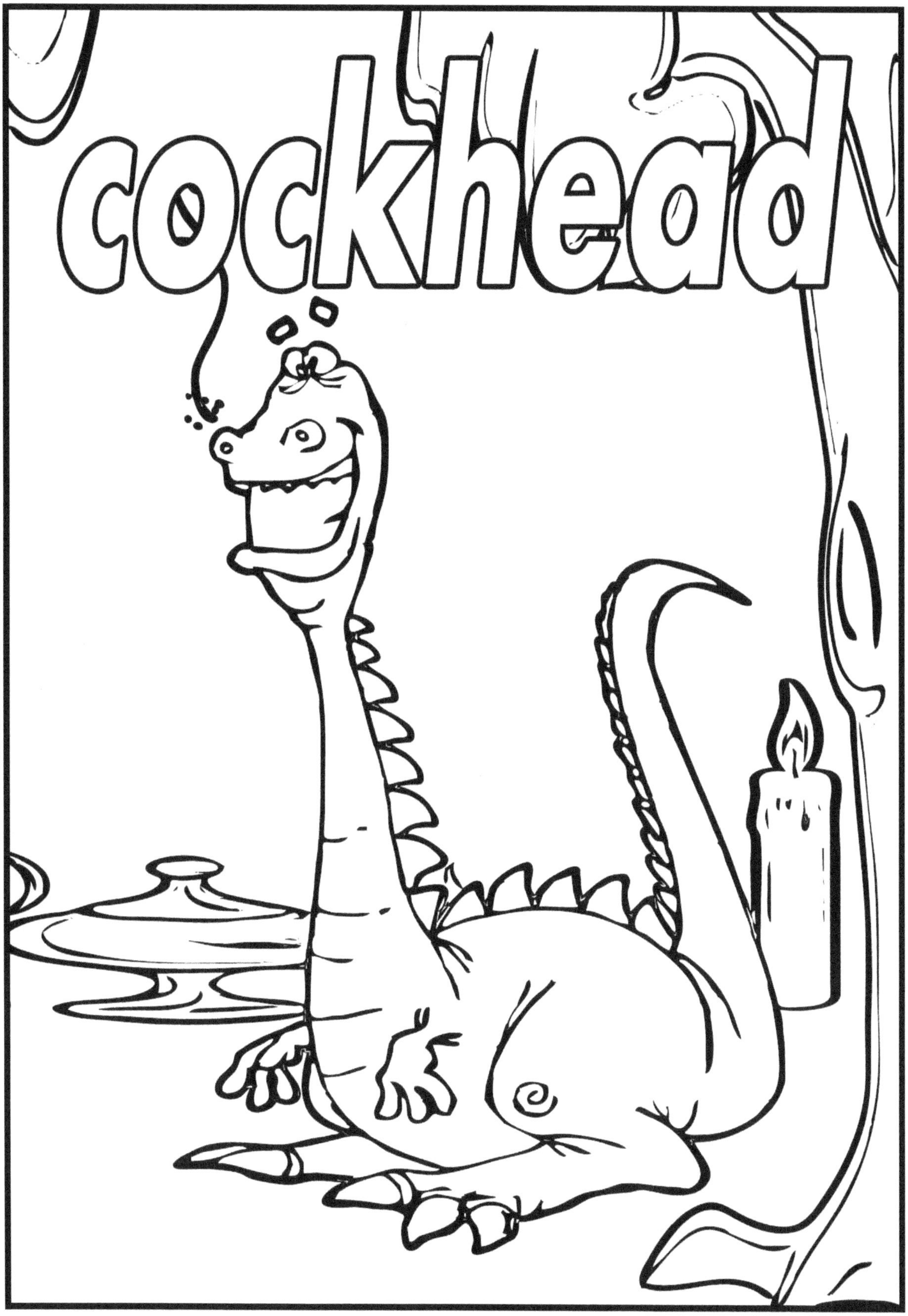
cockhead

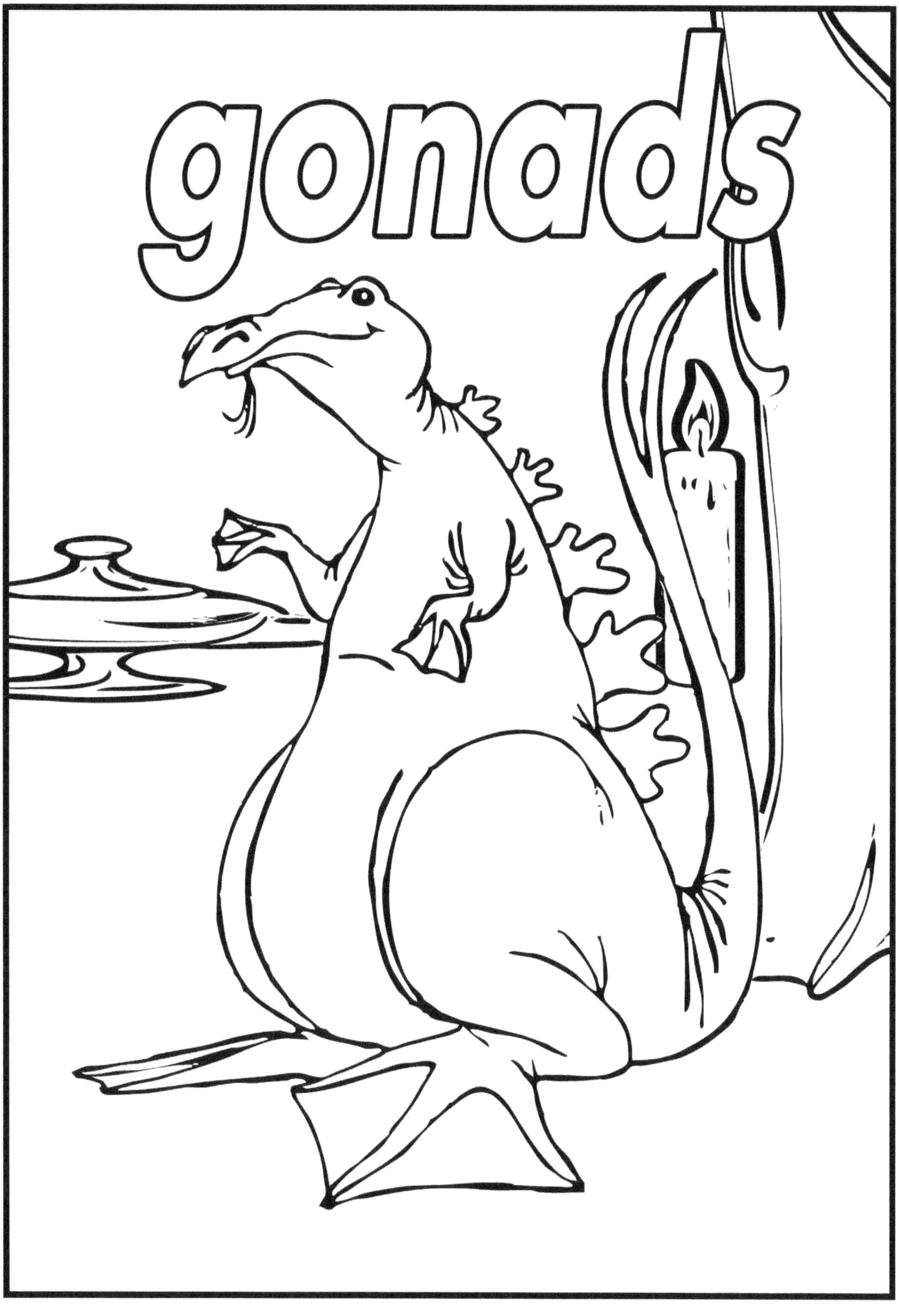
gonads

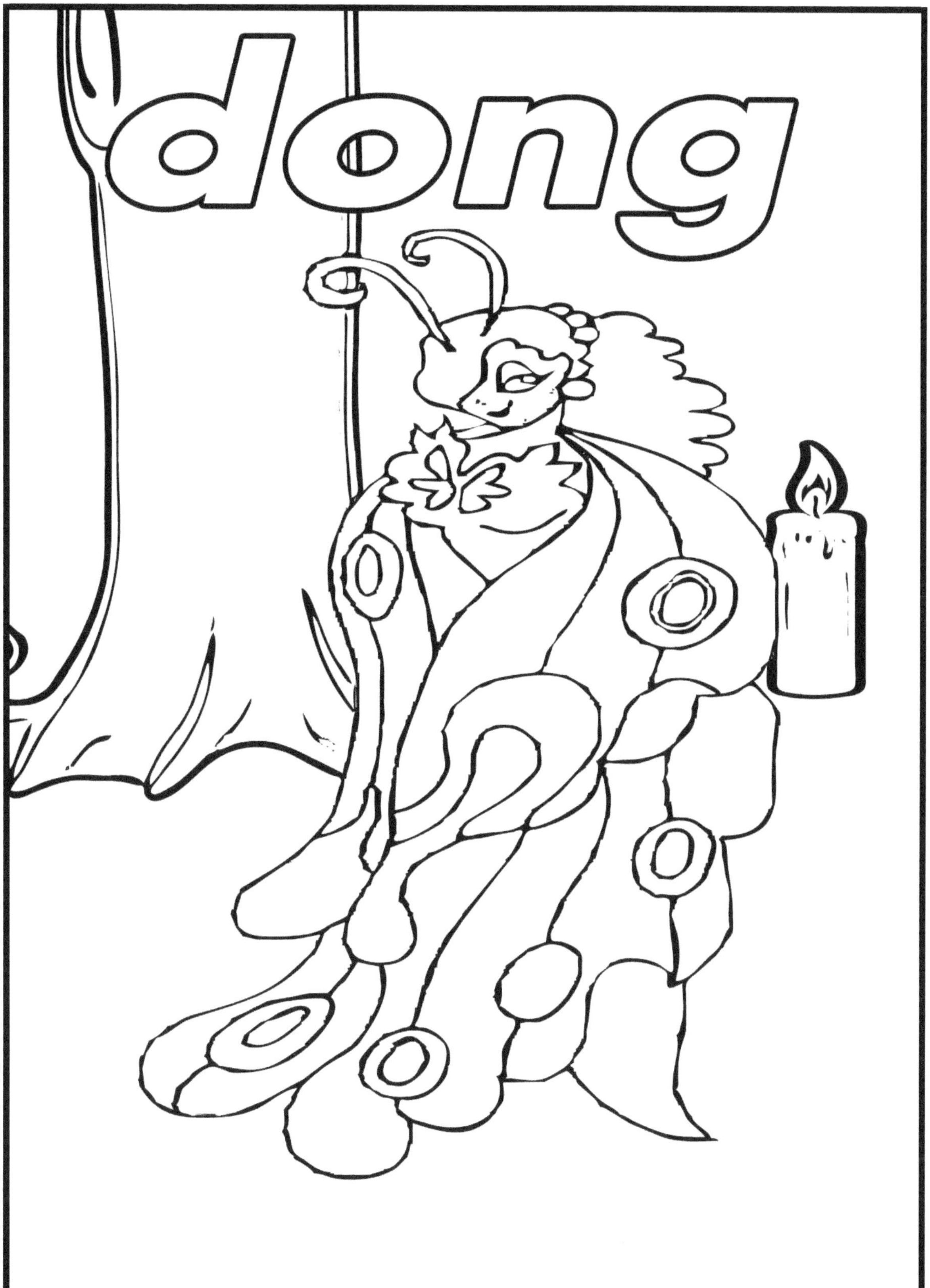
dong

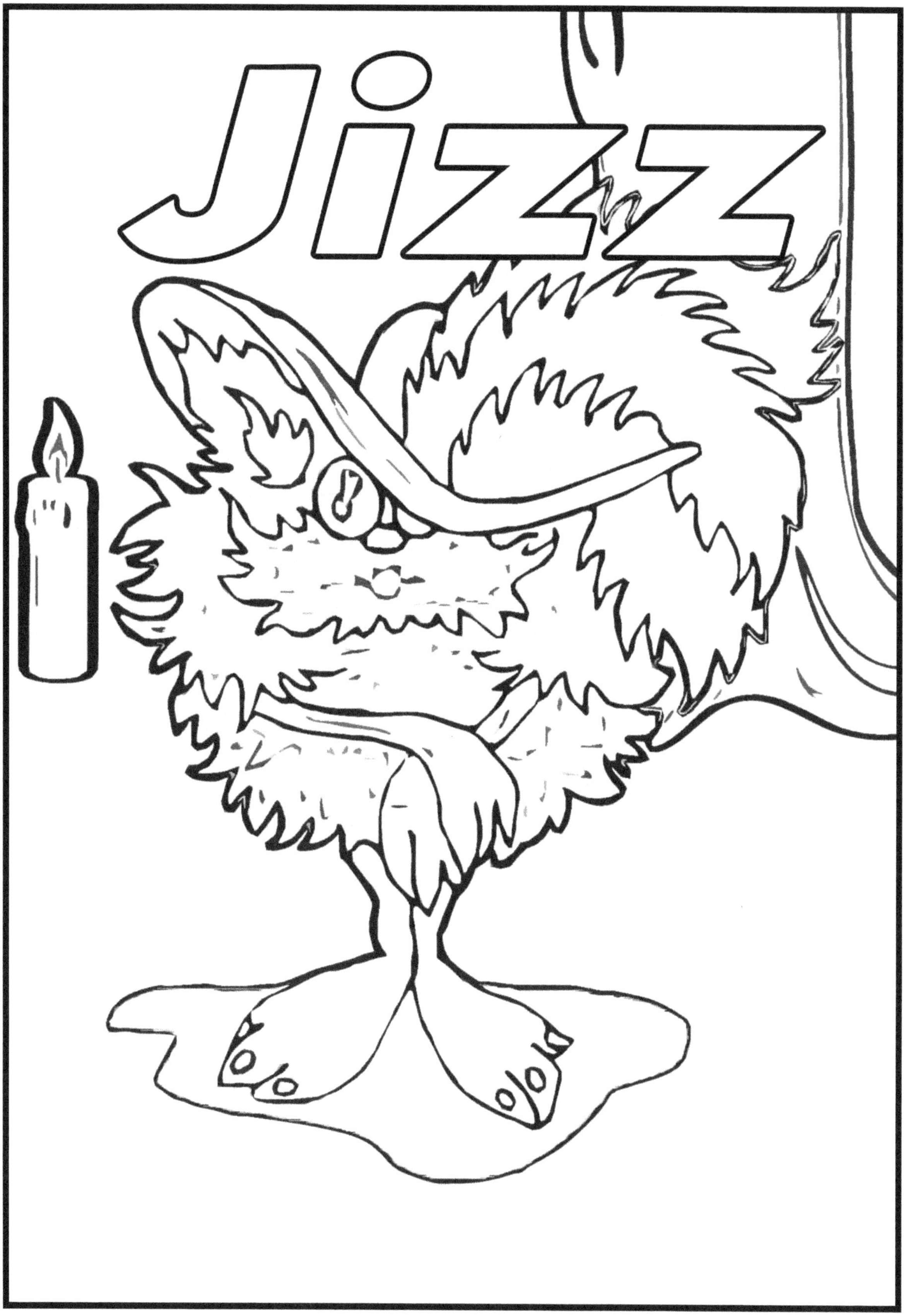
Jizz

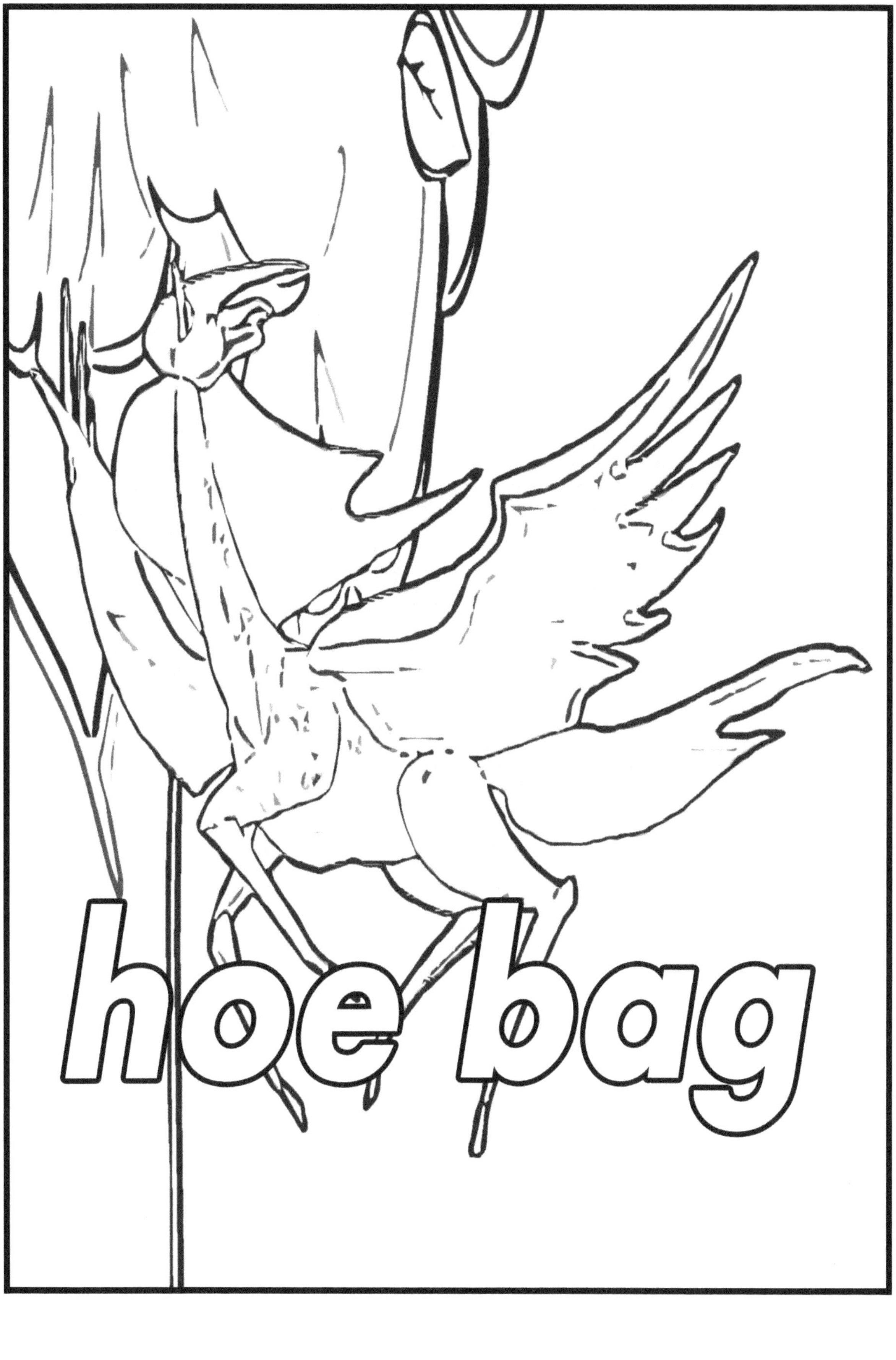
hoe bag

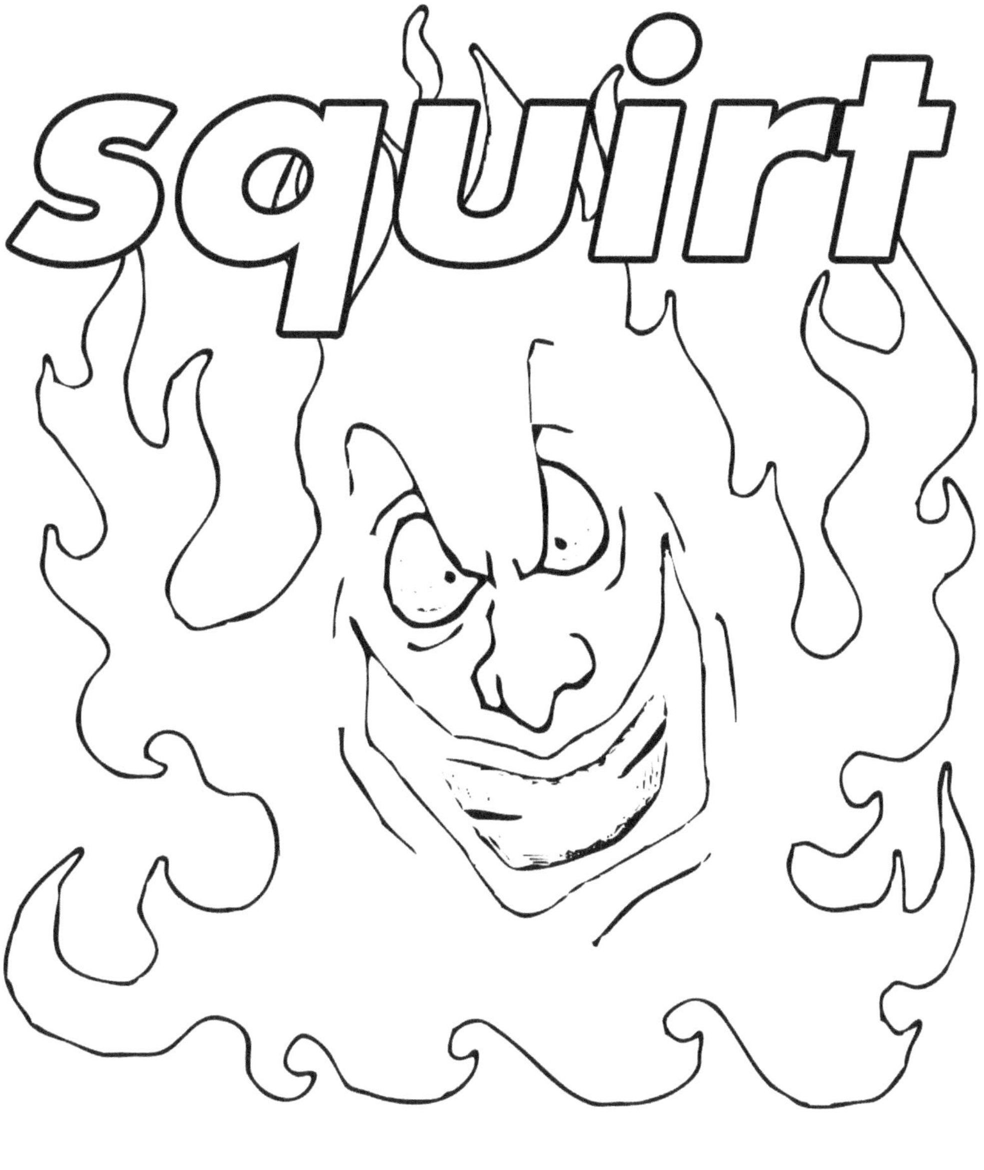
squirt

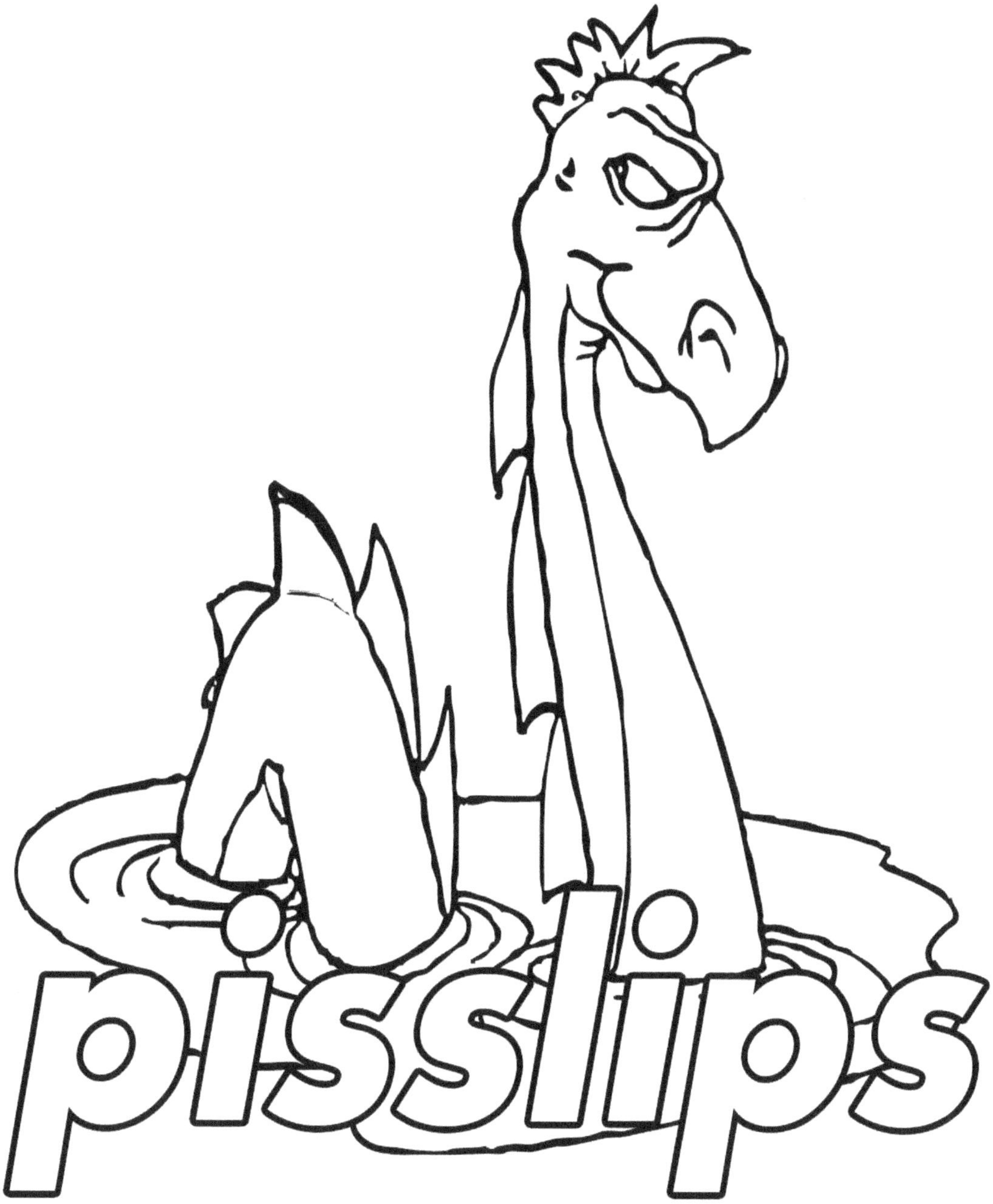
pisslips

www.ingramcontent.com/pod-product-compliance
Lightning Source LLC
Chambersburg PA
CBHW080612190526
45169CB00007B/2983